Grandad's Rock

Written by John Lockyer
Illustrated by Lynn Joubert-Mills

Eddie watched his grandmother stride along the path. "Come on," said Nan. "Let's go to the rock and listen to the sea." Eddie followed her slowly. He wasn't sure they should go.

Last year, after Grandad Joseph died, Eddie and his mum moved in with Nan. But, a few months ago, Nan started doing strange things. She got up at night and wandered outside. Sometimes she wore her clothes inside out and once Eddie heard her talking to the hat stand in the hall. His mum said her mind was drifting, so someone had to be with her all the time.

Eddie kicked a loose stone. It rolled along the path and stopped at Nan's feet. She stood with her hands on her hips. "You're so slow, Joseph," she said. "Hurry up."

Eddie sighed. When Nan was drifting, she often thought he was Grandad Joseph.

Nan grabbed Eddie's wrist and pulled him through the scraggly grass. "Joseph, when are you going to cut this grass?" she said. "If you wait much longer, you'll have to use the hay bailer. And the house, it needs a paint, too. It's time for action, Joseph!"

Nan dragged Eddie over the stile, then down the track to the beach. She moved quickly. Suddenly, she stopped and Eddie banged into her.

"What's wrong?" he asked

Nan turned and Eddie saw her eyes. They were bright and clear. She was back. "Where are we going, Eddie?"

Eddie smiled. This was the Nan he knew and loved, the real Nan. "We're going to Grandad's rock."

Nan looked at the beach and nodded. "Help me, Eddie." Her arm hung limply in his hand. Where was the strength he'd felt just moments ago?

Eddie led Nan carefully across the sand, stopping often for her to catch her breath. A large black rock stuck out from the cliff. Its base was worn smooth in the shape of a big seat. Nan and Eddie sat down. He hadn't been to the rock since Nan started drifting. It felt good to be there.

"My Joseph was right," said Nan. "No one believed him, but he was right." She pointed to the summer-brown hills. "Everyone in the family except Joseph wanted to sell all that."

Eddie slipped his hand inside Nan's. He enjoyed hearing her stories.

"Sell, we said. Split up the land and sell. All we could see were dollars." She laughed. "Lucky for us, Joseph had better eyesight. Boy, there were some fights; everyone yelling at the same time. Joseph just shook his head. He never got mad. His brothers did, though. But there was nothing they could do. The farm belonged to the family. It couldn't be sold unless everyone agreed."

Nan sighed.

"The fights hurt Joseph, though. Afterwards, he always came here to listen to the waves. This place calmed him. Then one time, after a really big argument, I followed him. I'd had enough. I wasn't going to let him run away to the rock. His stubbornness was ruining our future, or so I thought."

Nan pointed to the sand at her feet. "He stood there shouting at the sea. **'If we sell the land, we sell ourselves. I am not for sale! My children are not for sale! My grandchildren are not for sale! This land is where we belong!'**"

Nan coughed. "It was like he was having doubts and the only way to stay strong was to shout out his beliefs. I was just a few feet away. I felt tingles all over my body. Then he turned around and suddenly, away from the talk of money, everything he said seemed right. I don't know what it was. Perhaps it was this place. But from then on I was on his side."

Nan coughed again. "His brothers never understood. They wouldn't talk to us. In the end, they left for the city. They said, if we loved the farm so much, we could work it on our own. So we did. Then, after Joseph died, they tried to make your mother and me sell."

Nan laughed. "We said never and they got mad all over again. But Joseph was right. The family has been here for more than a hundred years and I hope we'll be here for hundreds more."

Eddie looked around. The sandy beach stretched for miles. In places, tall bush-covered cliffs rose out of the sea. Sheep and cattle spotted the fields. It was beautiful. He couldn't imagine living anywhere else. Perhaps that was why Nan had told him the story.

She patted the rock. "Joseph and I came here often, just to listen to the sea and talk." She put her arm around Eddie and pulled him close. "Just like us, Eddie."

Eddie led Nan back up the track. They were close to the stile when she suddenly gripped his arm and dragged him over the stile. "You're so slow, Joseph," she said. "Hurry up."

Eddie let her go. "Hey, Nan," he called out. "I think I'll get the mower and cut the grass."

Nan stopped and jammed her hands on her hips. "And about time, too. At long last we're going to see some action." She carried on up the path. "You can do the painting too," she called out.

Eddie smiled. I will, he thought. And, when I'm finished, I'll pull the weeds from the driveway, unblock the garage gutters and stack the firewood.

He smiled again. They were all jobs he knew he would have helped his grandad do.

Grandad's Rock is a Narrative.

A narrative has an introduction. It tells . . .

- who the story is about (the characters)
- where the story happened
- when the story happened.

Introduction

Who

Where

When — When Eddie went to Grandad's rock with Nan

A narrative has a problem and a solution.

Problem

Solution

Guide Notes

Title: Grandad's Rock

Stage: Fluency

Text Form: Narrative

Approach: Guided Reading

Processes: Thinking Critically, Exploring Language, Processing Information

Written and Visual Focus: Illustrative Text

THINKING CRITICALLY
(sample questions)
- What do you think this story could be about? Look at the title and discuss.
- Look at the cover. Who do you think these people might be and where are they?
- Look at pages 2 and 3. Why do you think Nan was doing some strange things?
- Look at pages 6 and 7. Why do you think Nan's strength comes and goes?
- Look at pages 8 and 9. What do you think "Joseph had better eyesight" means?
- Look at pages 10 and 11. Who is the man in the illustration? What do you think "I am not for sale" means?
- Look at pages 14 and 15. Why do you think Nan told Eddie the story?
- Look at pages 16 and 17. Why do you think Eddie is going to do all the jobs he talks about?

EXPLORING LANGUAGE

Terminology
Spread, author and illustrator credits, imprint information, ISBN number

Vocabulary
Clarify: drifting, hay bailer, stile, beliefs
Adjectives: *strange* things, *loose* stone, *scraggly* grass
Pronouns: his, her, they, she, it, you
Adverbs: followed her *slowly*, moved *quickly*, hung *limply*
Focus the students' attention on **homonyms**, **antonyms** and **synonyms** if appropriate.